M000087711

Surviving the Shun

Getting Your Head Above the Cold Shoulder

By Nancy J. Bailey

Surviving the Shun

Surviving the Shun

Foreword

I was prompted by a mutual friend to reach out to Nancy Bailey for possible submission of a foreword for this book. I am a Licensed Clinical Social Worker who has (among other roles in the mental health field) worked for a number of years in Child Welfare, as well as within the Correctional setting with adult males in a high security State prison. As I considered the task of writing a foreword, I reflected upon the fact that I have spent the majority of my career working with traumatized children, and that I am now, ironically, providing services to the adult "culminations" of these traumatized, abused children, who have unfortunately turned to substances, crime, and antisocial behavior, as as result of unresolved and often unacknowledged trauma.

As I read through this book for the first time, however, I quickly acknowledged within my own mind that this topic not only speaks to me from a clinical and professional perspective, but is quite personal to me.

I recall quite clearly a roughly two year period during which a group of girls took action to shun and mercilessly and aggressively tease me, every day, both ways, to and from school on our long bus ride. I am aware of FAR worse accounts of bullying/shunning, but I can speak from my own experience that their statements and actions shook me to the core.

Consequently, I concluded that people weren't all they had been cracked up to be.

So, years later (also ironically), I became a social worker. At some level, I wonder if I wanted to prove to myself that this takeaway message imprinted on me in my formative years was wrong.

Thankfully, I have been able to do just that. I do believe people are inherently good, but are often misguided. I also believe that there is ALWAYS a biochemical, as well as a behavioristic, explanation for the decisions and behavior of others. It also stands to reason that there is also a biochemical and behavioristic explanation for how we choose to respond to others.

I can sense that Nancy's aim in this book is to educate readers on the dynamics of shunning and bullying, but to her credit, she takes this a step further by explaining the neurological components to the trauma experiences of victims, as well as the behavioristic aspects of how the act of bullying/shunning is spurred on and reinforced by environmental forces. The author ensures that after reading, you will understand these dynamics in a way that will 1) help you to cope, 2) help you to heal, and 3) help you to extinguish the damaging behavior of others.

It's been said that "Hurt people, hurt people."

My hope is that this piece of writing can help you heal, as it has helped me, and that the cycle of interpersonal, projected pain, can finally come to its bitter end.

- Jamie Costner Zeeryp

Disclaimer

While this book contains real situations, the names of individuals have been changed to protect privacy.

If you are being shunned or abused in any way, please seek the help of a counselor or medical professional.

Wiktionary definition:

Breakaway

1. Having broken away from a larger unit.

   The **breakaway** republic is slowly establishing order and civil society.

2. Capable of breaking off without damaging the larger structure.

   a **breakaway** wall

3. (ice hockey) Occurring during or as a result of a breakaway.

4. (entertainment industry) Enjoying rapid popular success.

Prologue

You have every right to be mad as hell.

Victims of shunning are often the kindest, most mild-mannered members within a group scenario. Chances are you have done nothing wrong, and yet you still have been singled out for whatever reason…. Or maybe for no reason.

Probably, before the rage set in, there was bewilderment. As you are jettisoned into the outskirts of your social galaxy, you are floating helplessly in space, gasping for oxygen, wondering how you are ever going to get back to your green, normal planet.

People who were once a part of your life no longer speak to you. Or maybe they do speak to you, but they don't interact the same way. You are not included in group activities, not tagged in the office jokes, not invited to dinner with the girls. It's like you no longer exist.

There are few things more maddening, or painful, than being treated as if you are insignificant.

How do you make amends, reach out to those in power, make things right again?

Perhaps you have extended the olive branch a number of times, only to have it tossed onto a bonfire and doused with gasoline – while its olive rolls in the bottom of an arrogant martini glass.

If you are reading this, it is likely that you have passed the stage of shock and grief, and are moving into the anger phase of those who have been victimized by this heartless practice.

The hard truth is, once you have been shunned, there is no turning back. Even if you have experienced reconciliation, there will be a shift in the relationship. You are no longer equal. Those in power, who have done

14

this to you, may continue to assert their dominance or toy with your emotions.

So embrace your anger. Acknowledge it. There are ways to use it to fuel your recovery. You may feel like you're floating out in space, but you are not alone. Buckle up, because you are going to burn your way through this experience like a rocket hitting re-entry. When you land, your life will be completely different.

You will go on having better days, and they will be left with theirs. You won't need them anymore.

Chapter One
What Is The Shun?

According to Miriam-Webster, the definition of shunning is, "to avoid deliberately and especially habitually."

Nearly everyone has experienced the painful effects of shunning; whether being purposely left out of a group or pointedly ignored by an individual. The practice has become so commonplace within society, that it has been given different names. To describe the act, someone might say they ghosted you. Dusted you. Shook you off.

Anyone can attest to the pain of shunning. Not everyone can explain why it hurts so much.

In the film, "Ladybird", the explanation is simplified. There is a moment when a school counselor is talking with the leading lady, a role mastered by the elegantly natural Saoirse Ronan, about a paper she has written. The counselor remarks that it is clear how much Ladybird loves Sacramento.

Ladybird replies, "I do not love Sacramento. I was just paying attention."

The teacher replies, "What is love, if not attention?"

This is the theme of the movie.

At times, the attention featured in the movie isn't very loving. Ladybird's mother, played by the unabashedly cranky Laurie Metcalf, nags her incessantly, and often in ways that are cruel. In the beginning of the film, the arguments between mother and daughter escalate to the point where Ladybird jumps out of a moving car and breaks her arm.

It's human nature to argue and bicker with loved ones. Most of us know an old married couple who scold each other constantly. My mom and dad were notorious for this, their mannerisms and pitches on a level that would rival the parents of George Costanza.

"I've asked you and asked you and asked you!" Mom would screech.

"Well is it so hard to get up and come into the room and get my attention?" Dad snapped back.

"What would you do if I wasn't around? I could be dead. I could be dead!" Mom shrieked.

Their arguments often made no sense; trailing along like a broken road riddled with potholes. But this type of interaction keeps the synapses firing and in fact, it can help us live longer. Indeed, my parents both bickered into their eighties. They also shared many hours filled with laughter and companionship. During their last days together, they were still holding hands.

While squabbling can play a role in long term relationships, the finest personal interaction is one of humor and support. Science has proven that even plants thrive when someone gives them loving attention.

In short, attention equals love.

Withdrawing attention, therefore, equates to a lack of love.

It is a sad technique by humans to use attention, or the removal of it, as a weapon. People who are abused through negligence can have food and water removed, and they will die within days or weeks. But people who have love removed can live for years, all the while dying on the inside.

According to Encyclopedia Britannica, shunning is a "social control mechanism." One of the problems with The Shun is that it is so difficult to quantify. Because people simply dissolve, rather than resort to the

more typically understood bullying, defining it becomes
an exploration into the negative.

In one of the crueler aspects of the shunning form
of bullying, the victim isn't always notified as to what is
happening. People just begin to fade away with no
warning. The victim might notice first one person acting
strangely, and then another, and another. The phone
stops ringing. The presence on social media vanishes.
The victim, without notice, has been dusted like a rag
snapping out an open door.

Another method used by bullies is to use the
Shun as a threat. Folks with some type of leadership
position, whether it be in the office or in social groups,
can tell the victim what is about to happen. Perhaps the
subject is told to get in line, or else. And then, true to
form, the bully has his minions fall in behind him,
clustering in groups to rush over the proverbial cliff like
lemmings. The victim is left stunned, in a psychological
vacuum where there is no control, and nothing to fill the
emptiness.

Shunning is one of the most vicious conspiratorial tools used by social persecutors. Purdue University has produced research that shows ostracism as harmful as physical pain. The brain waves associated with shunning are identical to those of a victim who has been shouted at, beaten and otherwise abused. The results can be deadly. Many shunning victims resort to suicide.

It doesn't help that society today encourages the "walking away" from toxic individuals. Ostracism, or group shunning, is completely different from the politically correct "diss" of an abusive personality for the sake of self-preservation. Shunning can be a sectarian gang effort to single out one person who may or may not have done anything wrong.

Once shunning is acceptable within a certain group, it is frequently accompanied by other forms of bullying. A typical ringleader in the shunning effort will be afflicted with some type of personality disorder.

Often, it is narcissism. This can be combined with other issues such as addictions or other problems that can lead to insecurity. A narcissist can rationalize and may know that shunning is wrong, but he/she doesn't have the emotional chops to comprehend how it feels. A narcissist is devoid of empathy. It can be hard wrapping your brain around this, but you may know a person who walks and talks like a human being, while inside, he or she is a soulless vampire. Some narcissists are excellent mimics, and very charming, and it can be tough to pinpoint the disorder. If you are paying attention, somewhere along the way you will notice signs of a lack of empathy. Maybe he taunts a homeless person or is mean to animals. Take these signs as a big red flag.

Shunning can go hand-in-hand with discrimination. African-Americans, homosexuals and people of other nationalities are all too familiar with this way of life. Anything that marks you as different from some established norm can set you up to be shunned.

Unfortunately, shunning can be genetic! Some parents teach it to their children, either consciously or living by example.

Shunning is crazy-making stuff. Thanks to science, we are now beginning to understand the effects of shunning and ways to get past the damage it can cause. One of the problems with shunning is to understand when it is happening to you. Is the person ignoring you intentionally, or are they just preoccupied? Is the sudden cold attitude of others just your imagination? Is it them, or is it you?

Hopefully, the chapters ahead will help you understand the act of shunning and how you can recover, or even better, how you can escape from the grip of the Shun entirely.

Chapter Two

Why People Shun, And Why It Hurts

Like most adults who are single, I have been through a plethora of relationships. Many of the guys cheated on me. With one of them, I discovered another woman's underwear between the sheets on his bed.

Naturally, we broke up, following a trail of some household items that did not survive the shattering episode.

That guy – I'll call him Omar -- had mastered the art of passive narcissism. He was very good at ignoring people and acting superior. He would be sitting watching TV and when I spoke to him, it was like I was invisible. For a while I wondered if maybe he was having some kind of grand mal seizure. I eventually decided he was just horrifically rude.

Omar had driven his young adult daughter, who lived with him, to near madness. She used to wake up in the middle of the night screaming. He would go in and comfort her. It was very obvious to me why she was doing it. It was the only time she ever had his full attention.

Omar is extremely abusive, as both a father and a boyfriend. Because he wasn't hitting his daughter, or yelling at her, the terms of his abuse were difficult to pinpoint. He had damaged her terribly by ignoring her.

When we broke up, I was compelled to keep calling him. I would call him every day; sometimes several times a day. When he answered the phone, I would yell at him to stop answering when I called.

That's how crazy-making this guy was. It made the daughter, and now me, look like the lunatics. In retrospect, we were probably both just fine. It was him.

Omar had us conditioned to work for his system of intermittent reward. We were working our heinies off trying to get his attention. He was a master of this type of control, and he did it so skillfully that even after years of training animals, and employing the same principle, I never realized what was happening to me. The compulsion was so strong that it carried on after we broke up. On the occasions when he would look at me directly, engaging me, I would feel a sense of relief until the next round. After we broke up, I would feel temporarily assuaged through calling him, even if I got his voicemail.

Human behavior is weird. But this principle actually works on a very simple premise. So for those who have been shunned, but haven't found a way to stop engaging the Shunner, I offer this explanation:

Your Shunner Is Training You Like A Dog

Imagine yourself in a casino, sitting at an old-fashioned slot machine. You put the tokens in and pull

27

the lever. Usually, the symbols don't line up. But on occasion, they do, and you get a pile of change. If you are really lucky, you will hit a jackpot and earn a thousand dollars or more. The whole process is entwined with bright lights and colorful images. When you win, the bells ring and the words, "Jackpot!" flash in front of you. It is a sensory overload, and all very exciting.

The power of the slot machine works through the principle of intermittent reward. This type of reward system is more compelling than a constant reinforcement for the same behavior. The suspense of waiting, of never knowing what is coming, is like gravity, pulling you in to repeat the behavior again and again.

While training dogs with food, I ignore bad behaviors. Eventually they go away. But for behaviors I want to strengthen, I will offer rewards on a sporadic schedule, just like a slot machine. Once a dog learns to sit, if I want the dog to sit very quickly, I might give him a bit of food for just the fastest responses, ignoring the other times he just slowly lowers his rump to the floor. I up the ante each time, maybe offering him a jackpot, a pile of treats if he breaks his own speed record.

By giving me attention only part of the time, my boyfriend slowly trained me to keep making bids for it. This training was so powerful that it even extended into a phase after I found evidence of his cheating.

When you end a relationship with a Shunner, you may find your behavior escalating. You might be coming up with different ways to try to get their attention, or excuses to contact them. This, like my phone calls, is what trainers know as an extinction burst.

Imagine going to an elevator, hitting the button, and nothing happens. What do you do?

You hit it again.

It is not unusual for people to hit the button repeatedly before giving up. This is a perfect example of an extinction burst.

When people withdraw from you, and you continue to reach out, you are experiencing an extinction burst. Eventually, if the Shunner ignores you, you will give up. But if the Shunner gives you any encouragement at all, you are being rewarded intermittently and you will increase your efforts to contact him.

You can take control of your response to his training. Since the response to intermittent reward is deeply intuitive, you will need to identify what is happening. At that point, in order to break the cycle, you will have to treat it as if you are quitting smoking. The easiest way is to replace your habit with another habit.

With Omar, I took his number out of my phone and replaced it with my mother's number. Thus, when it slipped my mind and I had one more reason to shout at the guy, I'd wind up dialing Mom instead. That killed it!

Whether your Shunner intends to train you like a dog, or not, is beside the point. What the Shunner wants or thinks is no longer relevant. The important factor is your own mental health, and your path to independence from those who would control you.

Don't despair – what you are experiencing is a common phenomenon. You are human. By getting up in your head and addressing it from there, rather than simply reacting, you can overcome residual effects of the Shun.

Blame It On The Brain

When you are a victim of the Shun, your brain will respond in ways that are not nice.

Purdue University's Dr. Williams stated that the brain's dorsal anterior cingulate cortex (try saying that three times fast) is the part that registers physical pain, and it responds to ostracism in the same way. Your brain is making cortisol, the "stress hormone" produced by your adrenal glands.

Cortisol has its uses. It's a steroid hormone and when dispensed as a pharmaceutical, it's called hydrocortisone. It can help to lower inflammation.

But when your brain reacts to bullying, cortisol raises your blood sugar and suppresses your immune system. It can also reduce bone formation (excessive cortisol over the long-term can cause osteoporosis) and messes with your potassium. It can cause gastrointestinal issues, memory loss, and other problems. Too much cortisol is not a good thing. Stress is very hard on your body. Therefore, it is a good idea to understand the effects of ostracism in order to control your stress levels.

Dr. Williams explained that targets of ostracism typically go through three stages:

1. The acts of being shunned.
2. The victim attempts to cope.

3. The victim experiences resignation.

Williams designed some computer games in order to study the reaction of people to ostracism. Playing cyber-ball, wherein a ball was passed back and forth between several unknown players, the subjects were suddenly excluded from the game. Even when the subjects knew they were playing against a computer and not a real person, they still reported feelings of rejection, loss of control and lower self-esteem. Logging responses of over 5,000 people, Williams was able to prove how a mere two or three minutes of ostracism can produce lasting negative emotions.

During the second stage of ostracism, different targets reacted in different ways. Many of them made attempts to be included. They offered behaviors that were established as ways to be accepted, including submissive acts of contrition.

When the attempts to get back into the fold eventually fail, the targets may resort to lashing out.

After a long phase of ostracism, the victims eventually give up. Once a person lands in the resignation phase, they tend to be angry and depressed. For those who are upset about the loss of control, some feel an act of aggression will restore control, at least temporarily. Studies are showing that ostracism may be even more painful than other types of bullying, as it hearkens to a primitive instinct still rolling around in the ol' noodle. Basically, we as a species are family-oriented. We evolved by coexisting in groups. Therefore, if we are outcast from the group, there is no one to hunt with us or keep us warm. Outcasts do not survive. It is reasonable to understand why the reaction to ostracism is something akin to panic.

Modern humans do not have those same basic concerns, but the inherent need for companionship and acceptance is primal.

This deep social interdependence is what causes victims of shunning to be psychologically brutalized beyond other types of bullying. The resulting pain can make it difficult to bear, and many of them commit suicide.

Chapter Three

What To Do If You Are Shunned

Shunning is an ancient technique used by cultures, and even religions, since the beginning of man. It is a way to employ power over another individual. It is tribal in nature, its effectiveness depending on the human need for inclusion. But individuals use it too. Today's dependence on social media has put a whole new spin on shunning. If you unfriend someone on Facebook, you are shunning them. People joke about being unfriended, but the pain that occurs when it happens to you is very real.

So how do you handle it?

First of all, figure out what type of Shun you are dealing with, and how long it has been going on. When did you first notice something was wrong? Have you inadvertently been making bids to get the Shunner's attention? Has this manipulation been going on for weeks, months or even years?

Emotional abuse within a family, although common, can be the most damaging of all. Family is the backbone of your existence and is supposed to be an important part of your daily structure throughout your lifetime.

Many gay people can attest to the damage done by family shunning, because they endure it when they come out. Families may shun someone who has left their established religious group, or married someone the clan doesn't like. On other occasions, the reason for the shun may be more difficult to pinpoint, and there may be no reason at all. In my own family, jealousy played a major role. I had several sisters who were envious of me to the point of obsession, nearly rabid over my close relationship with our dad. After his death, they orchestrated a shun, spread lies, got the brothers involved, and soon the entire group of siblings dragged in cousins, nieces and nephews. Except for one brave and insightful sister, the whole lot was involved in a group shun against me.

The bottom line is, the Shun is all about control. It is a way to send a powerful message to the victim: "You are inferior." Where the entrapment begins is when the victim starts trying to figure out what they have done to cause this horrible treatment. Sadly, the answer is that sometimes there is no answer. The Shun is more about the Shunner than it is about the victim.

Most people who are shunned are not exactly sure what is happening at first, but they get a definite sense that something is wrong. The victim's reactions can escalate as the frustrations of being ignored begin to heighten.

Shunning incites rage.

The person who is shunned has a right to feel angry. It is difficult to quantify the act of shunning, as it is a non-act. How do you make a change in something that isn't there? This is why identifying the Shun, calling it out and addressing it is the first step in handling the issue. The victim should understand that, at one point or another, nearly everyone has experienced the Shun. It can start as early as kindergarten and extend into old age. Most of us know that gnawing feeling when someone is looking right through you. With many of us, this begins in childhood.

Families: Clan of the Cave Forbearers

Shunning within families is one of the most common forms of abuse and it is one of the most destructive. The urge to shun is deeply tribal and hearkens back to ancient days. Within some tribes, if someone in the family was weak or old, or deemed a burden to the clan, they were cast out.

One narcissist in a family can create a wake of destruction, especially if it is a parent. If the kinfolk are composed of more than one narcissistic personality, prepare to learn how to set limits.

Family members will often single out one scapegoat. There may be no real cause for this, other than it is a primal instinct to select the weakest member from a group. While the victim may not technically be the weakest, there might be something about them that is different. They could be smarter, kinder or better looking. Jealousy plays a huge role in family shunning. It's a pretty good bet that if you are being shunned by family members, resentment toward you has been simmering for some time. If you think back, you will probably have seen the signs, perhaps without even realizing it.

If your family is small, you may have an easier time breaking away from the grip of the Shun. You may have had to rely on friends for fulfillment and social interaction for years. But if you have a large and tightly bonded family, an organized shun can hit like a ton of bricks. Either way, the Shun can be devastating. Rest assured that you are not alone in this experience. No one can hurt you as much as family members, but there is life on the other side.

You may ask yourself, "What sin have I committed that would make this brother turn against me? What did I do to suddenly be treated as if I am dead to them?"

Nothing.

The answer is, there is no answer. There is usually some convoluted mess, or excuse. But it is typically based on nothing. No family should be torn apart by Shunners. Any person who values you at all does not resort to the Shun.

What can be extra difficult with family is that they never really seem to go away. It would be easier if they did. Once they find out that ignoring you is no longer a way to get your attention, they may resort to other tactics.

When Shunners start holding out hoops for you to spring through, it is different from a real attempt at resolution. A Shunner does not want an equal relationship. If you are expected to blindly follow orders, be aware of what is happening. It means that they are losing control over you. They are trying to get you back in line.

Looking for the answer as to why people so easily fall in line with the Shun, and trying to resolve the issue, will make you nuts. It is a trick; a game. Shunning is pure tribal mentality.

Do you feel like the black sheep, or the crazy one in the family?

It isn't you.

I urge you to make a list and address each person in your mind. As you write, some of the dynamics may become clear to you. You might understand who organized the Shun, who are the leaders and who are the minions. You will find that the negative facts will vastly outweigh any good thoughts about each individual, no matter how close you may have been. If you complete your list, writing it honestly, you will start to see qualities in your own family members that are not all positive. This will be your first step toward claiming ownership. You may experience a shift in your thinking, placing responsibility on them for their actions, rather than wondering how you have caused it.

There may not be a reason for any of it. An imagined slight is often all it takes. Shunners make up their own excuses for their abuse. Usually they are lies, or fabrications, or twisted facts. The hallmark of an abuser is to justify his behavior. Don't fall for it. You are the one who is wronged. A majority vote means nothing. Pack mentality is not rational.

It can be difficult to separate yourself emotionally and look at the bigger picture. This is where writing can help. If you stick to listing past behaviors, rather than feelings, you will begin to see the Shun for what it is: A heartless, vicious act of emotional cruelty.

This is where my history as an animal trainer has been of help. It has conditioned me to look for behaviors instead of words. I am a positive, reward-based trainer. I use very little punishment. But I am very firm about not giving in to manipulative acts. Dealing with Shunners is the exact same thing as working with an animal. It has helped me immeasurably with distancing myself on an emotional level, and watching the actions of my family from a purely behavioral perspective.

You might say people are not animals. Oh, yes we are. The act of the Shun is very primitive. Animals gang up on each other. Dogs in a pack will single out the weakest or the mildest-mannered individual. You should never leave a group of dogs alone together with a small one. No matter how many years they have lived together, if there is a dispute over a bone or a bed or a toy, there is a good chance that the big dogs will kill the smaller one.

If you live with a group of narcissists, they act the same way.

After my parents died, I had to write off nearly all the members of my immediate family. Out of six surviving siblings, I have only one remaining who is emotionally healthy, and she is the only one I still speak to.

Since I am normally a family-oriented person, this great loss, on top of losing my mom and dad, might well have devastated me. But it hasn't. I have survived the abuse, and I plan on thriving and having a magnificent life.

You can, too.

You don't have to stay tied to your family. You are under no obligation to associate with people just because they are genetically linked to you.

Shunning is an extremely toxic and contagious activity. It appeals to bullies, and it appeals to others because humans like being part of a group. But if someone is too weak to stand up to the crowd on your behalf, and is so willing to forsake a history of love and camaraderie, that person is a lost soul. You can no longer help them. It is time instead for you to take care of yourself.

Once your list is written, I urge you to go to all your social media sources, be they Facebook, Twitter, Instagram or whatever, and get rid of these people. You must delete or unfriend every person who is participating in this abuse against you. If you are tempted to stalk their page or try to find out what they are up to, or who is talking to whom, block them. This will prevent you from seeing their content. Erase every shred of them from your virtual existence, because believe me, they have already erased you.

This is your first step toward recovering from their bullying. It might hurt. In fact, it probably will hurt a lot. If it does, remember it is not you who has created this pain. You are tearing off the band-aid.

If cutting family off through social media seems spiteful, that is not the intent. Rather, the goal is to get control of your own mind, to nurture your health by turning toward more positive connections. With family, there is the unenviable task of deciding if you want to attend reunions. With weddings, graduations and other events requiring an invitation, that's a no-brainer. You may not get an invite. If one of the Shunners has been civil enough to invite you, it is appropriate to send a card with sincere congratulations. I would advise against attending the event. I would further advise strongly against sending the Shunner any gifts or money.

A funeral is another story. It might require some thought, but just do whatever is best for you. There is no shame in avoiding funerals. They are dreary occasions rife with human drama. The only redeeming quality about attending a funeral is the chance to catch up with people you care about, while your presence can be a comfort to the bereaved. You have to decide if it is worth the aggravation of dealing with the family Shunners. You can always send the good relatives and true friends a card or note, begging off and making a date to get together. If you feel strongly that you must attend, perhaps for the sake of someone innocent who might show up, see if you can enlist the support of a friend to go along with you. Having someone around to act as a buffer can help ensure that belligerent Shunners and obnoxious bullies behave themselves. A friend is also a great comfort to you at such a time.

You can make your own family. Yours will be one of love and support, not constant dysfunction and backstabbing.

Think of this time as a turning point in your life. Mark the date. Most people have lifetime events that they hail back to, which heralds a big change from that point on. It might be a marriage, or the birth of a child. Some people might say, "Before my surgery," or, "Before the house fire."

This is your life event. From here on, you are living in, "After my Breakaway."

48

Work: When The Gang Around The Water Cooler Freezes You Out

Shunning in the workplace is dirty business. It is highly damaging, but can be difficult to prove due to its covert and incendiary nature. The Shun is everywhere.

According to "The Social Outcast," by Kipling Williams and Joseph Forgas, different individuals react in different ways to shunning. It can be a humiliating experience to be excluded from the after-work drinks on Fridays, or not copied on the interoffice joke emails. The target can experience varying phases of depression, and anxiety. As the ostracism continues, these feelings build up over time. The employee is expected to continue to function on the job, full well knowing that the social games are carried out behind his back. Management is often privy to this abuse, but will do nothing about it. Or, worse, some managers will participate.

49

As I explained in the Prologue, rage is a very common and justifiable reaction to The Shun. But some individuals carry their anger one step further and become violent. This is demonstrated when the occasional news report covers a shooting in the workplace when a disgruntled employee goes bananas.

Think about who suffers most in these scenarios. Is it the Shunners? Generally not. It is the victims, and then more victims are created.

Violence is never the answer.

The answer lies in control.

When violence is the result of the Shun, it means that the target is reacting instead of coping. He or she has lost all sense of control.

If you are being shunned, it is best to pull your emotions out of your gut and get up in your head. Your survival – at least your emotional survival – depends on it. This can be tricky, especially since Shunning is proven to affect not only emotions, but the victim's cognition.

In other words, The Shun messes with your brain. Therefore, it is very important to be aware of your reactions to the environment. You might even consider transferring or leaving this job for one where you will be treated with more kindness. If this is not possible, there are ways you can control the situation, mainly through the way you respond.

The office can be a big drag, but you can cope with the abuse, and even thrive on it, by taking notes. Make small observations about the way people are behaving. Keep a journal. As you vent your frustrations through writing, their behavior will seem more ludicrous. A sense of humor can be a beam of light for you, and incidentally, everyone around you.

If you wish to reconnect with these Office Shunners, pick the one that seems the most humane.

51

Find a skill where he or she excels, and ask for help with something you are working on. Nothing softens a person like being asked for assistance.

From there, you can send a small thank you gift, or leave it on their desk. Select something funny like a bobble head doll or an amusing coffee mug.

If this small interaction doesn't open a door where you are treated more warmly, don't bother to pursue it. The intent of this book is not to help you find ways to placate Shunners. It is to show you that you are not alone in your experience, and suggest ways that you can be okay in spite of it.

In his book, "Ostracism: The Power of Silence," the author, Purdue's psychologist Kipling Williams explains the four human needs that fall under attack when a person is shunned.

1) The sense of connection and belonging.
2) The control between our actions and outcomes.

3) Self-esteem.

4) Being acknowledged; having an impact on our environment.

Studies have shown that people feel isolation very deeply, even in contrived situations that they know are temporary. Shunning can be extremely damaging. Professor Williams cites effects including ailments such as ulcers, anxiety, and a suppression of the immune system.

When shunning happens at work, it can affect your performance. Therefore, it is best that the Shun be recognized and labeled as quickly as possible, so that you know what is happening. You don't have to know why, because there isn't always a reason. But once the Shun is identified, it becomes easier to put a plan into action for self-healing.

First of all, you must understand that while the Shun says more about the Shunner than it says about you, the focal point is on YOU. Shunning takes energy. Every participant has a non-verbal contract and they all are immersed in a team effort. Do you realize how important this makes you? You don't even have to do anything to warrant it. The hostility is boiling up from them, not you.

When you get a handle on this, it becomes easier to see the ludicrousness of the shunning effort. You may even be able to get to the point where just thinking about it makes you roll your eyes.

There is so much power in that type of disengagement.

You can fulfill all four of your human needs that are swept up in the Shun.

1) Connection and belonging

   Consider outside activities to look forward to. It is so important to have friends and activities outside of the workplace. Your physical health is also crucial in reducing stress. Aerobic exercise and yoga can help you maintain your critical thinking, keeping oxygen feeding your brain. It will help you sleep. Nurture yourself.

2) Control

Since control is such a huge factor in dealing with the Shun, you may want to set up a rather rigid work schedule for yourself. Regulate every hour, and stick to it. If you can set aside time to go outside for a walk at lunch, by all means do that. An hourly schedule, checked off each day, will help you with a feeling of accomplishment. These may seem like small steps. But they will put your brain on the track to recovery. They also provide a level of comfort, as you have a ritual to focus on, rather than thinking about the barrage of silence from the office bullies.

Set goals for yourself. If you reach personal achievements each week, reward yourself with a favorite treat: a pedicure, or that dress you've been eyeing.

3) Self esteem

By taking care of the first two needs, self-esteem will follow. You will be your own best friend, your own inner light. You can begin by nurturing yourself. You are worthy of love. When you are able to give yourself this assurance, it shows. Others will see it. Whether they acknowledge it or not is up to them. If they do not, it is their failure, not yours.

4) Having an impact

This is where having interests outside the office come into play. Having an impact can go hand in hand with connection and belonging. If you join a group or club, you can make a difference in a plethora of ways. It could be anything from joining a softball league, to campaigning for clean water, to walking dogs at the Humane Society. Each person can do great things in a little time.

It's important to make a contract with yourself and practice some personal integrity with your commitment. Concentrate on your own well-being rather than trying to find ways back into the good graces of ungrateful people. It might be a little more difficult if you have to continue to deal with Shunners every work day. But if you practice good habits and self-care, you will find it getting easier in time. As you progress farther into your new life as a Breakaway, you might find yourself feeling more compassion than you ever have before. There is nothing like going through hardship to make the plight of others stand out more clearly.

Chapter Four

How To Prevent Shunning's Damage, To Yourself And Others

Once you recognize that you have been shunned, the first step in recovery should be to find a compassionate therapist who understands how devastating ostracism can be. They should be able to help you find some direction in maintaining your sense of control and self-esteem.

After therapy, the second step is to begin feeding your brain the juice it needs to alleviate your stress. You need endorphins.

Exercise

The Mayo Clinic declares that exercise is the best way to start.

Nearly any method of exercise can act as an effective stress reliever. Activity not only punches up your endorphins, but it provides an effective distraction from everyday issues.

The good news is that it doesn't have to be kick boxing. It doesn't have to be anything rigorous or sweaty or time-consuming. Aerobics are great. But so is yoga or swimming or even just a simple walk. If your muscles aren't perfectly toned at the moment, you can still break the hold of stress by employing a bit of exercise.

When you indulge in movement that elevates your heart rate even a little, it fires up the neurotransmitters in your brain. These endorphins will elevate your mood. If you make this activity into a daily habit, you will find that your energy levels increase while your mindset grows more optimistic. Regular exercise improves your mental outlook, helping you to relax and sleep better. It can increase your self-confidence and improve your ability to focus.

It's a good idea to talk to your doctor about the best exercise program for your lifestyle and body type. Don't make an extreme change. Increase your activity levels gradually. If you overdo it, you not only risk injury, but muscle soreness might kill your incentive to keep going.

A good rule of thumb is what the Department of Health and Human Services suggests, which is for each healthy adult to get 150 minutes per week of moderate aerobic activity, such as walking, or 75 minutes per week of vigorous activity such as running. These should be in addition to strength training twice weekly.

There are so many different ways to get moving that it's easy to pick something that you like to do. Bicycling is very beneficial, as is hiking. If you have a dog, you have the perfect partner for a plethora of physical activities.

The Mayo Clinic suggests selecting SMART goals in order to help yourself to stick with it. SMART stands for:

Specific

Measurable

Attainable

Relevant

Time-limited

Some people do better with a partner. If you have a friend to go with you to the gym, you have extra incentive to keep going. Find what lights you up the most, and make it part of your permanent lifestyle.

Meditation, Comfort Food and Aromatherapy

Practicing meditation is a good solution for reducing stress levels. Meditating can produce melatonin, the "superhero" endorphin that is so beneficial for so many reasons. Melatonin will boost your immune system, help you sleep, slow down aging, and helps to prevent cancer and other diseases.

There are many other natural ways to reduce stress. They include:

1) Listening to music.
2) Getting a massage.
3) Cleaning your closet.
4) Venturing out in nature.
5) Taking a bath in candlelight.

Eating also will produce endorphins that can be soothing. There is truth in the oft-referred phrase, "comfort food." It's best, of course, to choose foods that are known for their stress-busting qualities. These include:

- Avocados
- Asparagus
- Citrus fruits
- Blueberries

- Oatmeal

- Cashews or walnuts

If chocolate is your safe haven, choose the dark variety.

Dogs

Dogs are a wonderful gift; unsung heroes to the human species. They offer a happy greeting upon every arrival, a welcome snuggle, a guaranteed friendship. If you don't see yourself with a dog, you can borrow one or go to a shelter that has a dog-walking program. But dogs are not for everyone. If you are not willing to take care of another sentient being for the next fifteen years, you can move on the next section. However, if you already own a dog, or are considering adopting one, this is for you.

Dogs offer tremendous therapy as a source of unconditional love. They are also a magnet for relationships with other people. Owning a dog presents a huge variety of activities with benefits that are not only physical, but emotional and social as well. Cats and other pets are wonderful companions too, but I will concentrate on dogs in this case because of the exercise factor. There are few things as nurturing as taking your dog for a jaunt every day. Walking your dog for at least a half hour on a daily basis is not only good for the dog, but it's good for you, too. It will bond you with him, and the exercise makes him easier to live with, as it tends to alleviate many behavioral issues dogs can develop through confinement. Dogs tend to attract attention, so when you are out and about with them, it gives you a chance to meet new people. Dogs provide a great point of reference, and are a good incentive to stop and talk to people. You can make new friends in the pet store, or on the hiking trails, or in agility class. Dogs are tremendous vehicles for socializing.

Petting your dog produces serotonin, the "love hormone" that is released while cuddling. The physical contact with a dog, even the act of tossing a toy for him, will lower your blood pressure.

Your dog will add a routine to your day. A dog needs to be fed and walked, and needs a place to sleep, and daily doses of love and attention. This structure of having a dog in your household will offer you tremendous stress relief. If you choose to rescue a dog, you have the added benefit of saving a life, and making the days so much better for someone else. Dog ownership can raise your self-esteem in unexpected ways.

Having a dog with you can reduce anxiety. It is soothing to have someone else to care for. Dogs are very good at living in the moment! Your dog can help you appreciate a day, without worrying about yesterday or what will happen tomorrow.

Perhaps one of the dog's most important roles is to provide you with companionship. The all-important human need for another soul to love can be alleviated in great part by your dog. Coexisting with him can help you prevent illness and even prolong your life. There is inherent goodness in the simplicity of dogs, although some of them are not that simple. The intangible personhood, the individual character of a dog, can become as dear to you as any human family member. Dogs give back in ways that are unpredictable and cannot be measured. Most of them have an uncanny ability to "read" their owners. Some will know when to snuggle up close, others will invent ways to get you to laugh. With a dog, the love is not a one-way street. He will be your willing sidekick in any endeavor you choose. Life is always better with a dog.

The Greatest Love of All

Whitney Houston belted out a simple truth. Learning to love yourself is the key to overcoming many issues. Psychology Today urges you to:

1) Care about yourself as much as you do for others.

Think about that for a minute. If you saw someone in the street, getting ready to hit a dog with a stick, or grabbing and shaking a little child, what would you do?

You would step in.

And yet, when it comes to your own self-defense, you often suffer in silence. If you can step outside of yourself for a moment, and picture yourself as a good friend, it gives you a whole new perspective on what you will tolerate.

You would never sit by and allow a friend to talk about how stupid they are. Why, then, would you ever berate yourself? Keep your self-talk positive and encouraging, just as you would for a friend.

A shift in your perspective will help you regard yourself as your own best ally. When you teach yourself to think this way, you will begin to bloom in ways you never expected.

Treat yourself as if you are worthy of love, and you will attract love. With practice, you can become your own life coach.

2) Set limits: Make a list of behaviors you will not tolerate.

Do this as a follow-up to number one. Can you take some good-natured ribbing? Where do you draw the line between teasing and verbal abuse? Putting these thoughts down on paper will help you clarify behaviors that are questionable.

3) Do what you need to do to be yourself: Find the things that light you up.

Activities that make you happy, whether it's a vigorous game of racquetball or a quiet afternoon of embroidery, are the fuel that offer nourishment to your brain. Try to stay conscious of moments in the day when you feel the most content and serene, and do more of whatever incites these moments.

Don't underestimate the power in altruism. Help others. Find your calling. Volunteer at the humane society. Go to the library and read to kids. Visit a nursing home. Donate your old clothes to a charity.

The best way to help yourself is to help someone else.

Your brain is a resilient, phenomenal, miraculous organ. There are so many forms of self-care that this barely scratches the surface. But if you are experiencing a Shun, it is time to turn your attention away from the Shunners and look inward. Your road to well-being can start with the simple mechanics of treating your brain to the right type of chemicals. These may not have to be artificial or even prescribed medication. If you put yourself on a schedule, regulating your own path to healing, you may find that you will break away more easily than you imagined possible.

If You Are a Shunner

You are certainly not alone.

Almost everyone has shunned someone; be it through a group effort or alone. Shunning often occurs after the breakup of a romantic relationship. Some couples stay friends. But with others, a shun is the healthiest alternative.

I shunned my sister, a Rosanne Barr – type sister, years before all my siblings dropped out of sight. It was not a group shun and I did not request or expect the participation of any siblings.

I realized that "Roseanne's" toxic behavior had gotten to be too much for me at that point in my life. I was recently divorced, with a family of animals to feed, and a broken truck. I was trying to make a living selling art, and she came to my booth and made a scene loud enough for the whole community to hear. It was not the first occasion; she was notorious for being loud, belligerent and mean. Every encounter had me walking on eggshells. I just couldn't take it anymore. After consulting with friends who agreed that I should step away from her, I sent her a letter saying I was all done.

Thus began my Shun. At least I gave her notice, and I didn't just disappear. She circulated my letter to every living relative, and probably beyond.

At that point, I didn't care. I was actually relieved. Roseanne is exhausting. She is an energy vacuum.

But the Shun was a mistake. Not only was it cruel, and behavior unbecoming to me, it had dreadful consequences. It removed me from Roseanne's life, and worst of all her son's life, and therefore the positive influence I had on the two of them was gone. It flung her straight into the shadow of other mean-spirited siblings.

She grew even more angry, spiteful and vicious than she was before.

At that time, I did not give myself credit for having a positive influence. My act of shunning was in some ways a product of my own low self-esteem. I had just come out of an abusive marriage. The ex-husband made me feel like I was totally insignificant, worth nothing. In so many words, he even told me I was Nothing. When you think you aren't important, you believe it is okay to shun because your presence won't be missed all that much anyway.

That is such wrong-headed thinking.

We all make a difference.

I am not saying that we should be responsible for others. I am not responsible for what happened to Roseanne. But it would have been better for her, for my dad and for me too, if I had found other ways to cope with her; maybe regulating her to holidays and special events, making my excuses at other times. Taking her in smaller doses may have been a workable solution.

There are ways to set limits without causing harm.

Since that day at the art show, I have made a couple of attempts to reconcile with Roseanne, but I had let too many years slip by. She made a few sporadic attempts to be civil when we saw each other at family events, which I appreciated. But her age-old anger continued to eke out of her. In more recent years, she has done some extremely hateful things, including abusing our disabled sister and hurling hurtful words and actions at my father while he was on his deathbed. Since Dad's passing, Roseanne has burned whatever rickety bridge was left between us.

Before you close that door, think about the one you are targeting. Do you really want to cause that person harm? Shunning will do that to them. It can change them.

If you have been cajoled into participating in a group shun, I invite you to think hard about that, too. A group shun takes energy and it is not positive energy. It is a negative, ugly spin and it requires you to keep it up. It sucks you in, and once you are beneath that cloak of darkness, it is very difficult to break out.

What is it about this target that makes you want to cause irreparable harm to him or her? What makes you want to take part in a movement that could drive someone to a state of anxiety, depression or perhaps even suicide?

You also might want to give some consideration to the ringleader. Here are a few questions to ask yourself:

- What is motivating them to demand this of you?
- What makes them think it is okay to ask you to behave this way?

74

- Where did they get the idea that they can tell you what to do?
- Why do they think you have this form of mean-spiritedness in you?

If you think a Shun is temporary, and things will be resolved with the target someday, think again.

Time walks on. Years pass. When a moment is gone, it's gone.

A Shun becomes status quo and it takes a great deal of effort to break the habit of estrangement. The more time that passes, the more distance will divide you. You would have to be really dedicated to reconciliation to open the doors again. You might make progress if you send the target a snail mail letter with an apology, and suggest a meeting, along with your phone number.

A face-to-face meeting is a much better way to reconcile than through any other method.

Then, when you offer yourself up, prepare to wait, and be ready to hear crickets. The target may want nothing to do with you.

Rather than having second thoughts later, and having to go through all these efforts, it is better not to join in a Shun in the first place. You don't have to be forced into the middle of someone else's dispute. And there are tactful ways to diffuse the Shunner's insistence. Tell them you will think about it, and then just let the matter drop.

If you are afraid of this ringleader, or feel compelled to give them control over you, it may be time to ask yourself why. It sounds like this Shunner is the actual source of the problem for you; not the target.

Whether this Shunner is your boss, or a family member, or has some other type of hold on you, maybe you should reevaluate your position in the relationship. After all, you have to live with yourself. You would probably rather live in a way that helps to build people up instead of tearing them down.

If you are reading this, chances are you have some sense of how damaging shunning can be. Don't underestimate the damage caused by your own role in a shunning movement.

The popular school of thought is that it's classy to remain silent and just walk away from someone who offends you. But it isn't always classy. To inflict that type of stress, to make a person feel shut out while never telling them why, is not the adult thing to do. It is the opposite.

Even if the target has hurt you somehow, there are more peaceful ways to make a statement, and more gentle ways to communicate your disappointment.

Don't underestimate the damage caused to you by participating in a Shun. It is stressful and if you have any semblance of conscience at all, it can eat away at you for years. The act of shunning can affect your health.

Plus, you are aligning yourself with people who are cold-hearted by mutual agreement. You are choosing your community. Is that who you want to be?

You are valuable. There is only one like you. Your positive energy can be a beacon to others. Light yourself up and live by example.

As food for thought, check out this beautiful quote by Elisabeth Kübler-Ross:

"People are like stained-glass windows. They sparkle and shine when the sun is out, but when the darkness sets in, their true beauty is revealed only if there is light from within."

The Light In You

The world is filled with millions of people. In fact, there are way too many of us; more than what is good for the planet. However, it does leave an ample selection for relationships. There is a veritable cornucopia of opportunities to connect with other souls. This remarkable table of diversity is just waiting for us to explore. There is so much love, friendship, happiness and adventure ripe to be tasted.

It is imperative that we, the Breakaways, stay open to new possibilities. Thankfully, they are literally endless.

For those of us who are introverts, it takes energy to initiate a conversation. This is energy that we might not have, especially after a devastating, soul-crushing rejection. But there are ways to make it easier.

Think about the thing you like to do the best. Set aside the need for money, tasks to accomplish, and obligations. When you have nothing else to do, or need to just unwind, what is the thing that occupies your time? Do you like to knit? Draw pictures? Play an instrument?

That is your passion.

Nothing is too weird. I personally know people who collect and show model horses. They take the factory models like you get in the toy department at Wal-Mart, strip the original paint off, and then customize them, changing the position of the legs or giving them new heads or ears, manes and tails. They paint the horse with the intention of looking as real as possible – hair by individual hair. They enter them in competitions.

I know other people who love to be background actors in movies and for TV commercials. They have parties and socialize and talk about what famous actor they saw. Maybe Pierce Brosnan smiled at them or Drew Barrymore was close enough to touch.

Both of these hobbies have forged close and lasting friendships.

There are so many activities that offer ample opportunities to meet like-minded folks. Sign up for a class, or join a club, and you will be amazed at how quickly you will gravitate to others, and they to you. This is because the focus is on the activity; not deeds or possessions or past wrongs or agendas.

The important thing to remember is that if you are invited somewhere, go! Even if you'd rather hunker in your bed with a bag of banana chips watching reruns of Sex and the City, the biggest favor you can do for yourself is to get moving.

Altruism can be the key to good living. If your energy is focused on helping someone else, your soul is fed. You forget your own troubles and if someone is benefitting from your time, your self-esteem will grow and bloom. Volunteering covers a host of issues. Consider showing up to walk dogs at the Humane

Society, or join a group that gathers food for homeless shelters.

The Dalai Lama says that negative emotions are mainly related to two things:

1) Self – centered attitude.
2) Accepting reality as it appears.

He adds, "Since all negative emotions are very much based on appearances, once you realize nothing exists as it appears, that is the wisdom side, and then altruism is the antidote to self-centered attitude. So self-centeredness is one factor. And then the belief, grasping at things as they appear, these two things are the basis of negative, destructive emotions."

I think of this as empathy being the source of healing.

I didn't expect this book to be such a cathartic experience for me. I consider myself to be a very strong individual, but I admit that reliving some of these experiences has been heart-wrenching. I laughed and cried while writing it. I hope these insights will help you on your path as a Breakaway. The fact that you have read it, the thought of someone benefiting from my efforts, is already helping me. So, count me as one of your achievements into altruism! You have my deepest gratitude.

Other Books By Nancy J. Bailey

The North Side of Down – A True Story of Two
Sisters (a B.R.A.G. Award Winner co-authored
by Amanda Bailey)

Seven Days on Drummond

The Cure for Shyness – A Novel

Clifford of Drummond Island

Return to Manitou

Clifford's Bay

My Best Cat

Holding the Ladder – A Novel

The Sleeping Lion

Eagle Flier (co-authored by Al Cecere and Bob
Hatcher)

Fifteen Rules for Clicker Training Your Horse

Fifteen Rules for Clicker Training Your Dog

Fifteen Rules for Clicker Training Your Cat

Twenty Five Ways To Raise a Great Puppy

Made in the USA
Coppell, TX
01 May 2021

54684527R00052